**W9-BMJ-357**

Bilingual Edition

Let's Draw with Shapes™

Edición Bilingüe

Let's Draw a Horse with Rectangles

Vamos a dibujar un caballo usando rectángulos

Joanne Randolph
Illustrations by Emily Muschinske

Traducción al español:
María Cristina Brusca

The Rosen Publishing Group's
PowerStart Press™ & **Editorial Buenas Letras**™
New York

1

Published in 2004 by The Rosen Publishing Group, Inc.
29 East 21st Street, New York, NY 10010

First Edition

Book Design: Emily Muschinske

Photo Credits: pp. 23, 24 © Digital Stock.

Randolph, Joanne
   Let's draw a horse with rectangles = Vamos a dibujar un caballo usando rectangulos / Joanne Randolph ; illustrations by Emily Muschinske ; translated by María Cristina Brusca.
   p. cm. – (Let's draw with shapes)
Includes index.
Summary: This book offers simple instructions for using rectangles to draw a horse.
ISBN 1-4042-7502-9 (lib.)
1. Horses in art—Juvenile literature 2. Rectangles in art—Juvenile literature 3. Drawing—Technique—Juvenile literature [1. Horses in art 2. Drawing—Technique 3. Spanish language materials—Bilingual]
I. Muschinske, Emily II. Title   III. Series
NC655.R36318 2004   2003-009491
743.6—dc21

Manufactured in the United States of America

Due to the changing nature of Internet links, PowerKids Press has developed an online list of Web sites related to the subject of this book. This site is updated regularly. Please use this link to access the list:

http://www.buenasletraslinks.com/ldwsh/caballo/

2

Contents

Contenido

Draw a red rectangle for the head of your horse.

Dibuja un rectángulo rojo para hacer la cabeza de tu caballo.

5

Draw an orange rectangle for the neck of your horse.

Dibuja un rectángulo anaranjado para hacer el cuello de tu caballo.

Draw a big yellow rectangle for the body of your horse.

Dibuja un rectángulo amarillo grande para hacer el cuerpo de tu caballo.

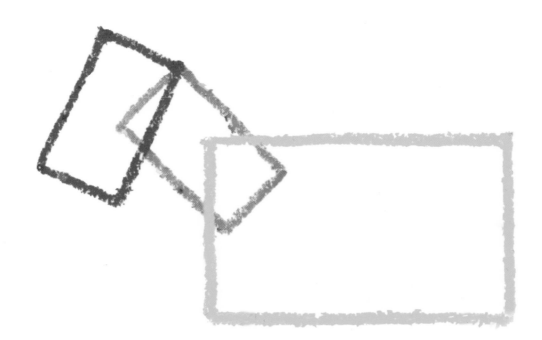

9

Draw two green rectangles for the legs of your horse.

Dibuja dos rectángulos verdes para hacer las patas de tu caballo.

10

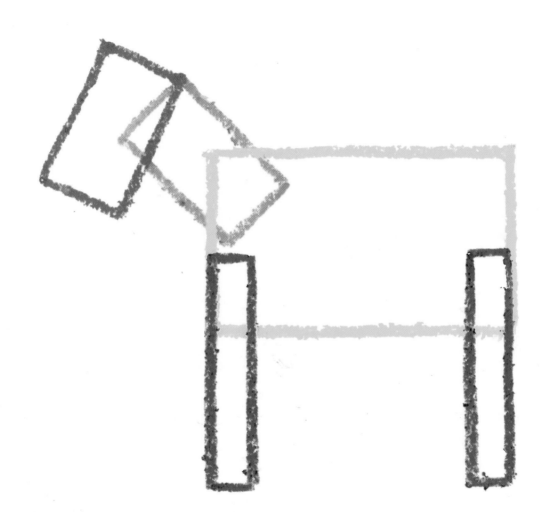

Draw a small blue rectangle for the ear of your horse.

Dibuja un pequeño rectángulo azul para hacer la oreja de tu caballo.

13

Draw four purple rectangles for the tail of your horse.

Dibuja cuatro rectángulos violeta para hacer la cola de tu caballo.

14

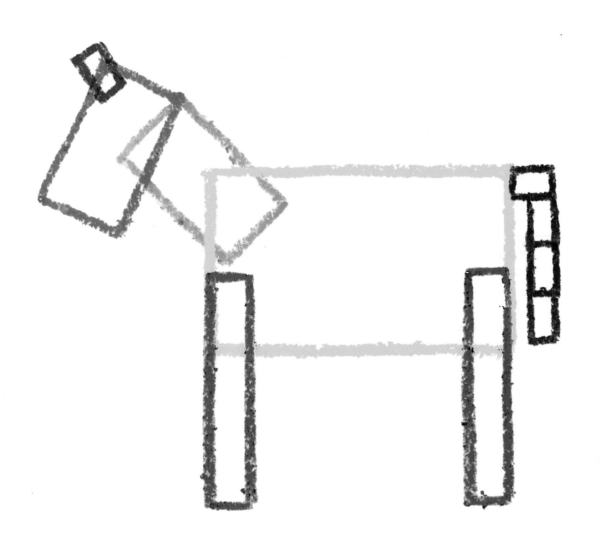

15

Add a pink rectangle to the head of your horse.

_____

Agrega un rectángulo rosa a la cabeza de tu caballo.

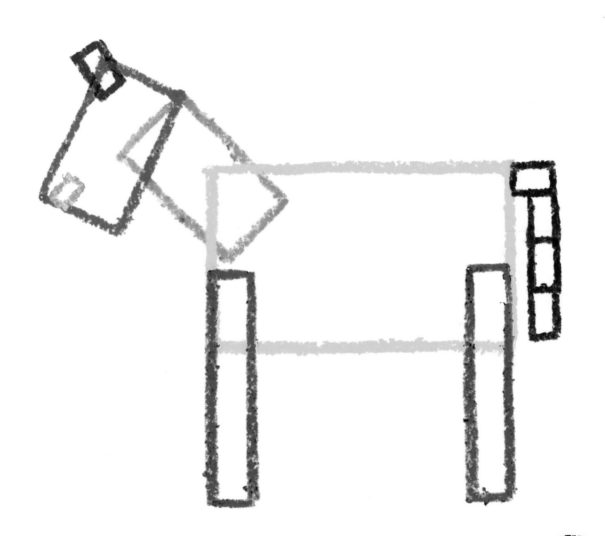

17

Draw a black rectangle for the eye of your horse.

Dibuja un rectángulo negro para hacer el ojo de tu caballo.

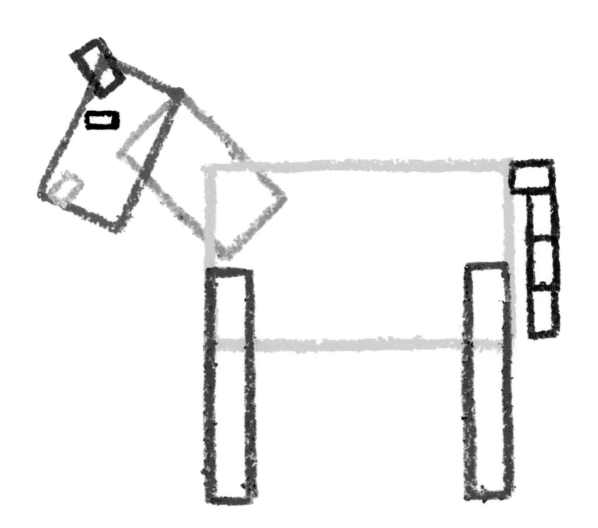

Color in your horse.

Colorea tu caballo.

Horses love to run.

A los caballos les gusta mucho galopar.

22

23

Words to Know
Palabras que debes saber

body
cuerpo

ear
oreja

neck
cuello

tail
cola

Colors
Colores

 red / rojo

orange / anaranjado

yellow / amarillo

green / verde

blue / azul

purple / violeta

pink / rosa

black / negro

Index

B
body, 8

E
ear, 12
eye, 18

H
head, 4, 16

L
legs, 10

N
neck, 6

T
tail, 14

Índice

C
cabeza, 4, 16
cuello, 6
cola, 14
cuerpo, 8

O
oreja, 12
ojo, 18

P
patas, 10

24